NOTES OF REFLECTION

Notes
of
Reflection

Scribbles on Life's Ups and Downs,
Words to Inspire and Grow

Irina Liechti

From my heart to yours

Introduction

The journey of writing this book began in the aftermath of a heartbreaking relationship. I found myself dealing with a mix of emotions – love, loss, hope, and the pursuit of self-discovery. Putting pen to paper became my therapy, a way to process the pain and find clarity. I've always liked to write things down, it's something I've been doing ever since I was a teenager. I jot down my thoughts, ideas, and I collect moments that inspire me, as well as memories that I cherish. These little notes were my motivation to be brave and solo travel the world, to pick up running and finish an ultramarathon and to remind myself that I can do anything I set my mind to. They were also a guiding light during my breakup and the period when I was struggling with self-doubt.

Life, with all its ups and downs, can be challenging at times. I hope my words will inspire you to confidently choose your own path and create a life filled with purpose and joy. Let these thoughts encourage you to embrace resilience in the face of difficulties and turn uncertainties into promising opportunities. May each turn in your journey become a new and exciting chapter of growth and happiness.

– Irina Liechti

Embracing resilience

When you feel down, remember storms don't last forever. Take a deep breath, acknowledge your emotions, but don't let them define you. Find comfort in small joys, in the warmth of a friend's hug, the smell of a morning coffee or the beauty of a sunrise. Reflect on past victories, remind yourself of the strength you hold. Practise self-care, nourish your body and mind. And most importantly, remember that every setback is a set-up for a comeback. So, stand tall, chin up, and keep moving forward.

You've got this.

Breakup

Leaving a relationship that doesn't serve you is one of the bravest things you can do. It's scary to imagine a life without the one you share everything with, yet incredibly liberating and powerful once your heart starts healing.

Acceptance

I try to accept what I can't change and keep my head
high when things don't happen the way I wish them to.

You matter

I want to remind you of something important – you are lovable. Yes, you! From the things that make you different to how kind you are, there are lots of reasons why people like you. You spread warmth wherever you go, making people smile. You're good at understanding others, which makes them feel safe around you. Sometimes you might feel unsure about yourself, thinking you're not good enough. But remember, those feelings aren't true. You are cared for, you matter, and you are loved. So, whenever you're feeling unsure, remember these words. You are loved a lot, just the way you are. Believe in that and it'll help you through tough times.

Letting go

It's a dangerous cycle of feeling broken when they leave and feeling high when they come back into your life, an unhealthy pattern that must be broken. Letting go of a love that isn't good for you is an act of kindness to yourself.

It's okay

Allow yourself to have a bad day, to cry it out and to sit with negative emotions. It's going to pass. Be gentle with yourself and give yourself time to heal.

Love

Love is supposed to make life better, not harder. It's like having a reliable friend by your side, someone who makes everything feel lighter. Sure, it takes effort and commitment, but it shouldn't feel like a constant struggle. With the right person, tough times become more manageable. They help you through life's challenges. So, don't believe the idea that love has to be painful to be real. Instead, know that it's meant to make life brighter, warmer, and happier. Trust in the idea of an easy love because when it's true, it won't be hard.

It's simple

Say what you think.
Share what you feel.
Communicate clearly.
Don't mess around with me.

Embrace all emotions

Not all emotions feel good, but the negative ones make us appreciate the positive ones.

Mixed emotions

I hate you for keeping me warm while you tried to figure yourself out. I hate you for never being satisfied. I hate you for comparing me to others. I hate you for constantly leaving and coming back. I hate you for never knowing what you wanted.

I love you.

Lessons

In life, challenging experiences teach us important lessons that eventually lead to better days. When we face difficulties, we learn to become stronger and wiser. Every setback helps us grow and understand ourselves better. Looking back, we see that hard times often have a positive side. They give us the opportunity to reflect on what truly matters to us. Although it's challenging, these experiences make us stronger and more determined. Difficult moments are valuable lessons, and they point us towards brighter days ahead.

Dance

When you feel sad, put on some music, listen to the beat, and dance.

You

You are beautiful.
You are smart.
You are strong.
You are brave.
You are kind.
You are loved.
You are enough.

Tangled emotions

His constant uncertainty drove me crazy, leaving me hurt and angry. Loving someone who couldn't make up their mind was exhausting. But even with all that frustration, I sometimes feel a longing for the old days. It's like I'm stuck in a loop of resentment and affection, unable to break free.

Hope

I was holding on to hope; hope that things would change, hope that he would change.

Self-respect

Remember, walking away may hurt for a while, but your heart will eventually heal.

Self-care

Light a scented candle.
Take a bubble bath.
Go for a refreshing walk in the park.
Buy yourself a new book.
Cook a delicious meal.
Bake yourself a chocolate cake.
Have a big scoop of your favourite ice cream.
Brighten up your home with a new houseplant.
Take yourself out for brunch.
Go for a relaxing massage.
Pamper yourself with a fabulous nail treatment.
Buy yourself a new outfit.
Treat yourself to a visit to the hair salon.
Book a holiday.

Roller-coaster

Life is a roller-coaster, without the downs we wouldn't appreciate the highs.

Memories

Sometimes I smile when I think of you,
sometimes I cry, and that's okay.

You rock

I just wanted to take a moment to remind you of how awesome you are. Seriously, you're pretty amazing. In a world full of highs and lows, you handle it all like a boss. Your strength and resilience? Impressive. You know what else? Your kindness and compassion don't go unnoticed. You've got a big heart, and you're always there for others. That's a quality not everyone has, and it's something to be proud of. Life isn't always easy, but you tackle it head-on. Whether you're laughing, crying, or dreaming big; you give it your all. And that's something special. Just know that you're not alone on this journey. I've got your back, cheering you on every step of the way. You deserve all the love and happiness in the world, so keep being your amazing self.

You rock.

Strong spirit

Life is tough sometimes, but so are you.

Learn to be alone

When you learn to be alone, you uncover inner strength and a deeper understanding of yourself. Spending time alone becomes empowering, encouraging personal growth, clarity, and the ability to approach life with confidence and authenticity.

Independent adventures

Quit waiting for someone to go with you. Go on that adventure you've been dreaming of alone. Travel by yourself, see new places, and learn about different cultures. Don't be afraid to eat out alone or watch a movie by yourself. Life is too short to wait for others. Enjoy the freedom of being independent and make unforgettable memories. Waiting for someone else might make you miss out on amazing experiences. Take a leap, try new things, and enjoy the excitement of exploring on your own.

She is

Gentle yet tough, reserved yet fearless, vulnerable yet resilient, flawed yet perfect.

Solo travelling

I've travelled alone so much that I sometimes forget how unusual it seems to others when I take a solo holiday. I used to get frustrated having to explain why I am by myself, but now I value these conversations. They remind me of how rare it is to enjoy one's own company. I've travelled alone for months, navigating through vibrant countries, adapting to new situations, and understanding cultural differences. When you are alone, there is no one to complain to when things go wrong. You learn to rely on yourself and handle obstacles independently. I feel fortunate to have the opportunity and courage to explore the world alone.

Introvert

I recharge my energy by spending time alone. It gives me the freedom to pursue personal interests without compromise. I enjoy peace and quiet, avoiding unnecessary drama and conflict. Socialising can be tiring, so I value my time and energy, choosing to spend it only with individuals who deserve it.

Nature

I love to be outdoors, surrounded by nature. Gentle sunlight shines through the trees. The air, filled with sounds from rustling leaves and singing birds, calms my mind. The light breeze and the smell of fresh pine make me feel revived. In nature, I feel at ease.

Mountains

It's a place where the noise of everyday life fades
away. The mountains teach me to be present, to
breathe in the fresh air and to appreciate the beauty
of simplicity. In the mountains, time seems to slow
down, allowing me to reconnect with myself and the
world around me.

Blessings

Life is not always easy but it's incredibly beautiful. There are so many things to be grateful for and we are so fortunate to be able to do what makes us feel most alive, to choose friends who make us laugh, and to build a life that makes us happy.

Joy in everyday moments

Each day, I take a moment to reflect on what I'm thankful for, starting with the comforting warmth of a cup of tea and the soothing water on my skin as I shower. When I leave the house, I practice mindfulness by being fully present in the moment, allowing myself to take in the sights and sounds around me, and appreciate the beauty each day offers.

I find joy in building meaningful connections with others and cherish spending quality time with friends and family. Engaging in activities that bring us closer together and having deep conversations makes me feel content. I value the bonds we share and treasure the laughter, support, and sense of belonging that come from these relationships.

I strive to be curious and explore new hobbies or activities that make me feel excited and happy. I find purpose in helping and supporting others. Prioritising self-care is important to me; I take care of my physical and mental well-being by nourishing my body with healthy food, exercising regularly, and giving myself permission to rest and recharge when needed.

Joy in life is often found in simple moments and in the love we give and receive. By focusing on what I am grateful for and embracing these values, I find that my days are filled with more happiness and meaning.

Life

Life can change in a split second, appreciate every day, do what you love the most, and smile often.

Grateful

…for spontaneous adventures.

…for moments of silence.

…for supportive friends.

…for the beauty of nature.

…for homemade meals.

…for my wonderful family.

…for heartfelt letters.

…for the thrill of a good book.

…for small acts of kindness.

…for my dreams and aspirations.

…for all the magic seasons.

…for chocolate ice cream.

…for the smell of fresh coffee.

…for warm showers and clean water.

…for finding beauty in the ordinary.

…for starry nights.

…for friendly strangers.

…for unexpected gifts.

…for the chance to explore the world.

…for people I can learn from.

…for sunrises and sunsets.

…for fairy lights and candles.

…for my favourite song.

…for a hot cup of tea.

…for the taste of summer fruits.

…for chocolate cake.

…for long walks in the park.

…for quiet mornings.

…for cosy nights in.

…for clear skies and sunny days.

…for discovering new hobbies.

…for the opportunity to live in different places.

…for time spent with loved ones.

…for the beauty of rainbows.

…for new beginnings.

…for comfortable shoes.

…for a white Christmas.

…for fresh sheets on my bed.

…for memories that make me smile.

…for autumn colours.

…for moments of laughter.

…for being alive.

A poem, written by me,
about the beauty we often fail to see

As we see the world each day,
its wonders seem to fade away.
The beauty around us, often missed,
the flowers, birds, by nature kissed.
The more we see, the less we find
and beauty fades within our mind.

Satisfaction

Life is beautiful and satisfying if you learn to appreciate what you have instead of constantly wishing for more.

Little things

Perhaps it's the little things that really matter. The fleeting smiles, whispered words, and gentle gestures. Perhaps it's the unnoticed details that hold the most significance.

Perspective

In the journey of life, it's easy to fall into the trap of thinking that the grass is always greener on the other side. We often find ourselves comparing our situations to those of others, longing for what they have while overlooking the beauty and value of our own lives.

But the reality is that things may not always appear as they seem. What may look perfect from a distance often comes with its own set of imperfections when we get closer. Just because someone else's grass looks greener doesn't mean it truly is.

Instead of always wanting more, it's important to be thankful for what we already have. Each of us is blessed with unique gifts, experiences, and opportunities that shape our lives in meaningful ways. By appreciating the richness of our own journey, we can find contentment and fulfilment right where we are. Concentrating on what we already have helps us to take care of it and enhance it, instead of always chasing after things we might never get. It's about finding joy in the present moment and making the most of the opportunities that surround us.

So, let's remind ourselves that the grass isn't always greener on the other side. Let's appreciate and enjoy the good things in our lives, and let gratitude lead us to real happiness and satisfaction.

Sunsets

There's something so special about the way the sky transforms into a canvas of colours as the sun goes down. When the sky turns shades of pink, orange, and purple, I feel like everything is alright in the world. Watching the sun set fills me with a sense of peace and happiness. Sunsets are magical moments that I adore because they remind me how beautiful and wonderful life can be.

Pause

We are living in such a frantic world, rushing from one place to the other on autopilot, completely forgetting to live and see the beauty this world has to offer.

The big picture

I could spend hours looking at the stars. I often wonder about the mysteries of the universe and what's beyond. It helps me put things into perspective. Suddenly, my problems don't seem so big anymore. The stars gently remind me that there's so much more out there beyond my worries, and that's a comforting feeling.

Moon

Pictures never do it justice, yet you'll still find me trying to capture the moon.

Mindfulness

Mindfulness isn't only about meditation; it's the ability to be fully present and aware of where we are and what we are doing. Have you ever left the house and forgotten if you locked the door? Or gone to bed and couldn't remember if you brushed your teeth? You can practise mindfulness every day without having to sit down and close your eyes.

Tranquillity

I feel peace when I step into the cold and look across the snow-covered field up into the mountains. With a coffee in my hands, I admire the sun rising behind the hills as the world slowly awakens. In this moment I feel alive.

High peaks and deep seas

I love the mountains, the fresh air, and the breathtaking views from the top of the summit. The mountains create a sense of calm, slowing down the rush of the world around me. Climbing up those rocky paths makes me feel strong and alive. I love the challenge and the feeling of accomplishment once I reach the top. When I am there, I find a connection to something bigger than myself.

But I also love the beach and the warmth of the sunshine on my skin. There's something magical about the sand and the sea. It's a place where you can let go of worries. Listening to the waves crash fills my heart with joy.

Awakening

Often, we are stuck in our bubble and the world we've been born into. We live in the same place, with the same people, doing the same job, and pursuing an interest we've had since childhood. But we never question whether all of this still makes us happy.

Wandering souls

Is it only me or are there others out there conflicted about where they belong?

There's this feeling of restlessness, an urge to break free from the comfort of the people closest to me and the places I call home. There's a voice in the back of my head, telling me to explore the unknown and discover new horizons in the hope that I'll find a place that truly resonates with who I am.

At times, it feels like I'm searching for a place that may not even exist. A place where I can be both rooted and free, where I can fully be myself, and where I belong without losing myself in the process. The more I explore and travel, the less I feel like I belong anywhere. But at the same time, I feel strangely connected to everywhere. The world is my home, and it's a blessing as much as it is a curse.

Perhaps, discovering who I am isn't about finding one specific place where I belong. It's more about understanding that I can change and adapt, that I can find comfort in the always-shifting world around me.

Ice cream

The solution to melt away stress and bring happiness.

Food is your friend

Food is the fuel that powers our bodies and minds. In a world often fixated on diets and restrictions, it's important to remember that food is not the enemy; food is our friend. Instead of viewing food with fear or guilt, let's see it as something that gives us energy and makes us strong.

Food is the foundation of good health, supporting our immune systems, improving our focus, and increasing our overall well-being. When we eat well, we feel well. So, let's celebrate food for what it is: an essential ally in keeping us energised and healthy. Let's appreciate every meal as a chance to fuel up, feel good, and stay strong.

Body love

Love your body unconditionally. Embrace its curves, scars, and imperfections. Nourish it with kindness, exercise, and wholesome food. Celebrate its strength and resilience. Your body is your home, treat it with the care and respect it deserves.

Be kind

Taking notice of the small acts of kindness people do for you will make you realise how much good there is in the world. Try it yourself and you'll be surprised. Being kind is free, and our world needs more of it, so here is a list of kind things you can do today to make the world a better place.

- Compliment a stranger
- Hold the door open for someone
- Start a conversation with the cashier at the shop
- Hug your friend to show you care
- Smile at someone
- Donate old clothes
- Send a letter or postcard to an old friend
- Give something you don't use away for free
- Leave an encouraging note for your flatmate

- Tell a friend that you appreciate them
- Volunteer
- Send someone a message just to say hello
- Bake cookies for your neighbour
- Buy your mum a thoughtful gift
- Tell your parents you love and appreciate them
- Buy someone a coffee
- Do not complain about anything the whole day
- Bring in doughnuts for your co-workers
- Tip a waiter you wouldn't ordinarily tip
- Call your sibling to check in
- Brighten up someone's day with flowers
- Cook a meal for your parents
- Leave a kind review for a small business
- Let someone go in front of you in line
- Compliment a co-worker on their hard work

Failing forward

If you succeed at everything you attempt and never experience setbacks, you're not reaching your true potential. Set bigger, bolder goals for yourself, because failure is a crucial part of growth and success.

Growth

You aren't failing, you are growing.

Never stop learning

Learning a new skill is hard, especially as an adult. Too often, we are afraid of making a fool of ourselves when trying something new, or we are too lazy to put in the effort and become impatient if we don't see results immediately. We feel most confident in our comfort zone, but that's not where growth happens.

I choose to get uncomfortable. I love to challenge myself in order to grow and become better, and I thrive on pushing through the hard moments. Because staying in the comfort zone and watching from the sideline isn't fun.

The journey of learning can be hard, with setbacks and moments of self-doubt, but it's these challenges that create the way for personal development and resilience. Overcoming obstacles not only builds competence in a new skill, but also encourages a mindset that welcomes constant improvement. Let's embrace the discomfort and face the uncertainties, because it's in those moments of struggle that we truly find our potential.

Healing path

Don't go back to what continues to hurt you simply because it's familiar or because you miss it. Healing isn't possible if we keep revisiting places that cause us pain. To heal and find peace, we must move forward, leave behind what holds us back, and embrace new beginnings.

Adaptation

I prefer adapting to your absence over feeling frustrated by your presence.

Stay single

Stay single until you meet someone who thoughtfully opens the door for you, someone who says, 'Text me when you're home safe', and stays up patiently until they know you are.

Stay single until you meet someone who holds your hand shamelessly and will kiss you in public, someone who pulls you close and gently kisses your forehead.

Stay single until you meet someone who wants to introduce you to their parents, someone whose friends already know about you and how special you are before you even meet them.

Stay single until you meet someone who drops everything to be there for you when you really need them, someone who genuinely cares and truly listens to what you have to say.

Stay single until you meet someone who doesn't try to change you, someone who doesn't compare you to others and loves you the way you are.

Stay single until you meet someone who asks about your family and the things you love the most, someone you'd proudly introduce to your parents.

Stay single until you meet someone who doesn't have time for games and is always honest, someone who keeps their word and texts back no questions asked.

Stay single until you meet someone who takes responsibility for their actions and knows when to apologise, someone who seeks to understand your perspective and values your feelings.

Stay single until you meet someone who sends you flowers to your office, just because, someone who sends sweet texts in the middle of a meeting they know you're stressing over.

Stay single until you meet someone who makes you want to be a better person, someone who motivates you to achieve more, supports your ambitions, and stands by your side even when things get tough.

Stay single until you meet someone who is sure of you and never makes you doubt how they feel, someone who is certain of their feelings for you and a future they want you to be part of.

Stay single until you meet someone who surprises you with your favourite coffee on a random Tuesday, someone who remembers the little details you've shared and makes an effort to show you they care.

Stay single until you meet someone who makes you laugh until your stomach hurts, someone who brings joy and lightness to even the most challenging days.

Stay single until you meet someone who says, 'I love you' first, someone who never stops trying to keep you, because they know that getting you wasn't the hard part; the real challenge is constantly giving you a reason to stay.

Until then.

Stay single.

Never forget

You deserve someone who chooses you over anyone else, someone who would give the world to be with you, someone who appreciates you, someone who admires you, someone who loves you.

Indecision is a decision

Mixed signals can be confusing. I've come to realise that indecision is actually a decision in itself, a way to hold back from commitment. I was left hanging and wondering where I stood. Today, instead of waiting endlessly, I focus on setting clear boundaries, because I understand that my time and emotions deserve respect.

This heart of yours

It's meant to be loved dearly, with passion and honesty, not to be broken.

Mindset mastery

Belief, hope, and positivity attract good things. Negative thinking invites what you fear. Your mindset shapes your reality. Embrace belief, stay hopeful, focus on the positive. It's up to you to steer your life.

Morning routine

Wake up early.
Have a glass of water.
Watch the sunrise.
Write down your thoughts.
Enjoy a cup of tea.
Move your body.
Go for a walk.
Read a book.
Nourish your body.
Be consistent.
Be patient.
Feel the change.

Progress

Don't forget to look back and see how far you've already come.

Sources of happiness

When we fall in love, it's natural to prioritise our romantic relationship above everything else, often neglecting time with friends, family, and our hobbies. However, relying solely on a partner for our happiness can leave us feeling shattered when the relationship crumbles. It's important to remember that our happiness doesn't just come from one place. Sure, romantic love is significant, but overlooking other parts of our lives can leave us feeling unbalanced and unsatisfied. So, while we're enjoying our romantic connection, let's not forget about the other things we love. By giving attention to all these areas, we can build a more complete and fulfilling life. It's about finding a healthy balance.

Choose well

Choose your company wisely and let go of those who dim your light.

Vulnerability

I used to find it hard to open up about how I truly felt. Putting on a brave face is a mistake I've made in the past. I've frequently dealt with difficult situations by myself, but I've come to understand that true strength isn't about bearing burdens alone. Strength is about recognising when you need support and having the courage to ask for it.

Friends

Choose friends who cheer for you and celebrate your success.

The front row

It's vital to understand the power of your inner circle, the individuals in your front row, the ones you can trust without hesitation. Knowing who they are and caring for this support network is key. These people are our pillars of strength, offering support, advice, and guidance.

Surrounding ourselves with a front row we can count on is essential in overcoming challenges, making important decisions, and leading with strong confidence. We need to choose our front row wisely.

Celebrate others

Being happy for others when they succeed doesn't take away from your own happiness or opportunities. Celebrating their achievements adds positivity to both of your lives. Remember, there's plenty of success and happiness to go around for everyone.

Success

If you want to be successful, surround yourself with
the type of people you want to be.

Passion

I never understood why people run… now I do.

My sanctuary

Running has had a huge impact on my life, and I've come to realise how much it benefits my overall well-being. When I run, it feels like a form of meditation, helping me clear my mind of worries and anxieties. It naturally improves my mood and boosts my overall outlook on life.

Running allows me to reflect on my goals and aspirations, and often, I find solutions to problems that seem overwhelming. It opens the door to new ideas. Through running, I have learnt to be resilient and persistent, which has encouraged me to stay disciplined and focused in various areas of my life. It taught me how to keep going and stay strong when things get tough.

At work, the focus I've gained from running helps me manage tasks with clarity. Whether I am managing projects or making critical decisions, I rely on the same dedication and endurance that get me through a long run. Through running, I've found a supportive community whose encouragement has played a big role in my journey of self-improvement.

Running is my therapy, my sanctuary, and it's teaching me valuable life lessons. It has empowered me to confront the things that scare me while improving both my mental and physical health.

What is your sanctuary?

Winning

Too often we make the finish line (for any goal) the win and we forget to enjoy the journey and celebrate how far we've already come. The real marathon is never just the race, but the preparation leading up to it. Winning is showing up every day.

Grit

Running is where I draw my strength from, the highs and lows of a race are what makes it worthwhile. As a runner, you have to push through some hard moments to get to the rewarding point. It's the same for life.

Racing

Crossing the finish line of a race you've been training for is one of the best feelings ever.

Marathon

My legs were aching, my knee throbbed with pain, I felt mentally drained and physically exhausted. Yet I kept going. And when it was all over, I found myself thinking I could probably do it all again.

Inner strength

You are stronger than you think you are.

Remember

Pain won't last.
You can go further.
Comfort is a lie.

What's stopping you?

And then I realised: nothing is stopping me but me. I'm in charge of my success. Only my own doubts and fears can slow me down. If I believe in myself and stay determined, I can overcome anything and reach my goals.

Feel the fear and do it anyway

It's okay to be scared but that doesn't have to hold you back. Just do it, even if you scream the entire time.

Just do it

Take that chance,
start that business,
change that job,
get those shoes,
wear that bikini,
forgive that person,
talk to your crush,
move to that city,
write that book,
go on that date,
take that trip,
live that life.

The choice is yours

One year from now, you'll either look back on a year full of excuses or celebrate a year of progress – it's up to you.

One day

One day I will pursue my dreams and take action towards my goals.

One day I will confront my doubts and replace them with determination.

One day I will overcome my fear of failure and step out of my comfort zone.

One day I will welcome challenges and see them as opportunities for growth.

One day I will silence the inner critic that holds me back from starting.

One day.

Today.

Discomfort

Learn to get comfortable with being uncomfortable.

Step up

Challenge yourself often,
push your boundaries,
embrace the discomfort,
don't forget to enjoy the journey.

Courage

How do you know your limits if you don't test them? How do you know what brings you joy if you don't go out there and explore? Be curious! Have courage! Life is exciting and it's beautiful, you just have to be brave enough to shape it the way you want.

Trust your vision

When pursuing your goals, you'll encounter sceptics who label your ambitions as too hard, too risky, or too overwhelming. They're likely projecting their own doubts onto you. Don't buy into their negativity. Stand strong against their doubts. Trust in your abilities and your vision.

Challenges are just hurdles to overcome, not barriers to stop you. Remember, many great achievements were once seen as impossible. Stay focused on your goals and silence the doubters with your determination. When others warn you about the difficulty ahead, listen to your gut – the one that says, 'You can'.

Self-confidence

Once you start to believe in yourself, you will reach heights that you thought were never possible.

You can

End of story.

Instinct

Trust your feelings, listen to your inner voice. Sometimes, your instincts know things your mind doesn't. Follow your gut; it helps you find your way in life.

Clarity

Don't sacrifice your happiness and inner peace for a relationship that doesn't feel right. You shouldn't constantly have to question where their head is at, whether they love you or not, and worry about when they are going to leave again. Doubt is a sign you shouldn't ignore; it's like your brain already knows but your heart wants to hold on. Stop lying to yourself. Sooner or later, it will break you.

Wrong love

I was in love with the wrong person for too long. I wasn't brave enough to leave what I deep down knew would never make me happy. I held on to something that drained me and brought me pain. I had hope. I was in love. In love with the wrong person.

Boundaries

Learning to say 'no' is essential for setting healthy boundaries, prioritising self-care, and respecting your time and energy. When you learn to say 'no', you unlock the power to shape your life according to your values and goals.

Liberation

Sometimes the most powerful thing you can do is walk away and choose yourself.

Reality check

I over-idealised the person I was with constantly. I was holding on to the idea of what we could be rather than what we truly were. We were a couple with different ideas of a great relationship and contrasting wishes for the future. Just because he was a good person doesn't mean he was good for me.

Moving on

I look back and know I have done all I can – I have loved with all my heart. If they don't know how to appreciate that or simply can't love me back, then there is nothing I can do. I have to respect myself and move on.

Self-worth

If someone is unsure about you, stop trying to win
them over. Don't compromise yourself any longer by
being someone's maybe.

Commitment

Choose to be with someone who is committed to you daily, not just when it suits their mood or desires.

Recognition

So one day I woke up realising how much better I deserve.

Peace

And then I felt a sense of peace. I am moving on. It's a weird feeling but somehow freeing.

Freedom

I can do whatever I want; I can read my books whenever I like, and watch whatever I fancy. I cook whatever I enjoy, go to bed, and get up whenever I want. If I want to travel away for the weekend, I will. I have time for myself and the things I love. I am free.

Flourish

When I stopped thinking about dating, I started to concentrate on my goals. I like how much I achieved because of it.

Singlehood

Being single rocks! No drama, no compromises. Just me and my goals, living life on my own terms. I've never felt happier. No need to deal with relationship complexities. I'm free to focus on myself. Being single isn't lonely; it's incredibly empowering. I enjoy my own company and appreciate the chance to explore my passions without distraction. Happiness isn't dependent on someone else; it comes from within. In this phase of my life, being single isn't a setback – it's a win.

Wanderlust

Travelling has a way of transforming us, creating a deep connection with others who share the same experiences. It's a bond that's hard to explain to those who haven't felt it. This is why, after our first adventure, we crave the next one. They call it the travel bug, but it's really the desire to return to a place where you're surrounded by people who understand what it's like to leave, grow, explore, and then come back feeling more lost in your hometown than you did in the most foreign place you visited.

India

Before travelling to India I researched extensively about the country – where to go, how to behave, and what to expect. I was advised, as a woman, not to travel alone to India. However, something drew me to explore this fascinating country.

While waiting for my flight to Kolkata at the airport gate, I sat next to an Indian family. We had a wonderful chat and I ended up playing games and sharing sweets with their daughter. Eventually, boarding started, and we said our goodbyes.

Tired and hungry, I arrived in Kolkata. I was about to buy a sandwich and water when the father from the family I met at the gate approached me, insisting on paying for my meal. I told him he didn't have to do that, but he replied, 'You made my family smile, you talked to my daughter even though she didn't understand you. Languages might be different in every country but a smile means the same everywhere.' And with this heartwarming encounter, my journey in India began.

Smile

Some people may not speak your language, but a smile is universally understood, it's the global language. Even if you can't communicate verbally, you can always share a smile together.

Impartial

This little girl suddenly sat on my bed on a night train to Delhi, talking to me for hours. She spoke Hindi. I spoke English. We didn't understand each other but the conversation went on and on. We ate cookies together, we made friends.

I love how children don't care where we are from, what religion we have, and what language we speak. When we smile; they smile back. When we are nice to them; they are nice back.

Curiosity

See the world through the eyes of a child.

Varanasi

Varanasi is perhaps the most fascinating and interesting place I've ever visited. Known as one of the oldest inhabited cities in the world and the holiest place in India, Varanasi is a sacred destination where cremation ceremonies take place.

Walking along the Ganges River, you inevitably witness cremations taking place openly on the ghats (the steps leading down to the water). I saw firsthand how families bring their deceased loved ones to the ghats, often arriving in cars or public buses. They gently wash the bodies with the Ganges' sacred water before the cremation. The process itself lasts a few hours, after which the ashes are respectfully scattered into the river.

What struck me most was the simplicity and acceptance with which death is treated here. It's not hidden or feared; it's a natural part of life, embraced with deep spiritual belief. Witnessing this made me reflect on how differently we approach death in Western cultures, where it's often seen as something to be hidden away.

Another powerful aspect was seeing how deeply people believe in the Ganges River's ability to purify, despite its pollution. The contrast between their spiritual beliefs and the environmental issues made me think about how we connect with nature and our responsibility to take care of it.

Varanasi's wisdom about life and death stays with me. It reminds me to value every moment and find beauty in life's darkest moments.

Discovery

Travelling is a great teacher, going beyond what you can learn in school. It helps us learn about different cultures, histories, and ways of life that you won't find in textbooks.

When we travel, we learn to handle new challenges and solve problems on the spot, like figuring out how to communicate in a foreign language or navigate unfamiliar places. It also teaches us to be more independent, making decisions about where to go and how to get there.

Travelling isn't just about practical skills, though. It also opens our minds to new ideas and experiences. Seeing different places and meeting people from different backgrounds helps us understand and appreciate diversity.

Most importantly, travelling humbles us. It shows us how big and varied the world is, reminding us that our way of doing things isn't the only way. It's an ongoing journey of learning, connecting, and growing – one that teaches us more about ourselves and others than any classroom ever could.

Beauty

Life is full of beauty; notice it!

A special place

Living in the beautiful city of Danang in Vietnam was a wonderful experience. Staying there for a few months allowed me to deeply immerse myself in the local culture and discover the city beyond its typical tourist attractions. Danang is a stunning coastal city with white sand beaches that are often empty since locals tend to avoid the sun. I loved spending my afternoons sipping Vietnamese iced coffee at a beachfront café, watching the waves roll in and soaking up the peaceful atmosphere.

It's close to the national park and the Marble Mountains, making it a paradise for an outdoor enthusiast like myself. The city is also very near Hoi An, a must-visit destination known for its colourful lanterns and rich cultural heritage. Hoi An is one of the most beautiful towns I've ever been to, and having it so close to Danang made living there even more magical.

But what made my time in Danang truly special were the people. The local family I lived with, their two wonderful children, the students I taught, and the friends I made all contributed to a memorable experience. Reflecting on those moments fills me with nostalgia. Danang holds a special place in my heart, and I miss this city dearly. One day, I hope to return to that wonderful corner of the world.

Your path

Have confidence in yourself and the path you decide to take. Not everyone will always agree with your choices and that's okay. You are not asking them to follow you and don't need their approval.

Moving abroad

Moving to another country alone, with little knowledge of the language, no job or accommodation, and no one I knew there, initially felt like an overwhelming hurdle. However, this leap of faith ended up sparking my personal growth and self-discovery.

From simple tasks like grocery shopping to finding a place to live, every step required resilience and adaptability. With each obstacle overcome, I discovered a powerful source of inner strength I never knew existed.

Taken away from all familiarity, I had no choice but to bravely confront my fears and insecurities. I learned to fully embrace discomfort as a path to growth and became an expert at finding creative solutions to unforeseen problems.

Additionally, being alone gave me a chance to think deeply about myself and what I really wanted in life. Removed from the influence of familiar faces and societal expectations, I freely explored my true passions and aspirations.

I eventually established myself. I secured employment, mastered the language, and made meaningful connections. But more importantly, this experience made me a more self-assured individual, capable of thriving when faced with tough situations.

Step by step

Just focus on the road ahead and keep on going.

You do you

This is a reminder to confidently do the things that make you happy, regardless of what others think.

Embrace yourself

You're great just the way you are, regardless of the opinions or judgements of others. Your worth isn't determined by external validation but by who you are inside. Embrace your flaws, quirks, and imperfections, they make you unique.

Remember, it's not about adapting to others' standards; it's about honouring your truth and living in alignment with your own values. Love yourself and accept yourself for who you are. Your journey is yours alone and true happiness comes from embracing your individuality.

Embrace yourself fully, including the parts that are still growing and evolving. Life is a journey of continuous learning and transformation. Allow yourself the space to evolve into the person you aspire to be. Celebrate your progress and give yourself permission to dream big, because you have endless potential waiting to unfold. Surround yourself with those who appreciate you for who you are, uplifting and empowering you to shine brightly in your own light. Believe in yourself, because you have a special kind of strength and beauty that no one can take away.

You're already good enough, just as you are.

I wasn't brought into this world to be what others want me to be.

Trailblazer

Celebrate being called 'weird' or 'different'. It means you're breaking boundaries, challenging norms, and daring to dream big. Let your uniqueness shine and inspire others to see the world differently. Keep being authentically you.

Ambition

Dare to dream so boldly that others question your sanity.

Evolve

Change makes us grow. When we accept change, we take chances, see things differently, and try new things. If we remain unchanged, we don't move forward. Don't be afraid to transform. Staying the same won't bring success.

Against the flow

Dare to go right, even if everyone else goes left.

Finish the sentence

I have always wanted to…
I am secretly afraid of…
This week I would enjoy doing…
I often look forward to…
Something the future holds for me is…
I get my strength from…
I would never…
It made me feel great when…
I love when…
It makes me angry when…
Something I deeply desire is…
I flourish when…
I find it hard to admit…

Simplify life

Do what you love.

If you don't like something, change it.

Stop over-thinking, it's often not that complicated.

Open your mind, arms, and heart to new things and new people.

Travel often, getting lost will help you find yourself.

Take risks and face your fears.

Life is one big adventure.

Single in my thirties

I've found contentment and fulfilment in my single life, appreciating the freedom to pursue my own interests and goals without compromise. Yet, despite my independence, I can't shake the subtle pressure of the ticking inner clock. It is as if society's expectations have crept into my subconscious, whispering reminders of supposed milestones I should be reaching.

I cherish my independence and the countless opportunities it offers, yet I can't ignore the occasional longing for companionship and genuine connection, leaving me wondering if I will ever find someone who's truly available and compatible. Finding a partner who's both down-to-earth yet driven to achieve their goals is certainly not easy.

I deserve someone who appreciates me as I am and highlights my qualities, offering mutual respect and consistent support in pursuing our dreams. I hold on to a sliver of hope that when the time is right, the universe will bring me together with someone who's waiting for a connection just like I am.

Harmony

Your outer world shines when your inner world is calm.

The complexity of love

As we get older, finding the right person can be really hard. When we were younger, love was the main thing we looked for in a relationship. But as we grow up, things get more complicated. It's not just about having feelings or chemistry anymore; it's about being a good match in many different ways. Now, it's important to be on the same page. Do we want the same things in life? Do we see our future together in a similar way? It's about finding someone who shares our dreams and values. The older we get, the more we understand the importance of finding a partner who not only makes our heart race, but also truly understands who we are. We change and grow, and it becomes harder to find someone who aligns with who we are becoming. Love would be easy in a perfect world, but this world is far from perfect.

Faith

When you are in your thirties, your friends have babies and the men you find interesting are already married. You sometimes can't help but overthink and wonder about the future.

I'd like to think it's natural, especially as a woman with goals and dreams beyond having a family of her own. Yet, I have to remind myself that I am exactly where I am meant to be. I am happier than ever, and I wouldn't want my life any other way.

So relax, enjoy, and trust the process.

Trust life's journey

What if you believed that all obstacles were placed in your path to help you get where you are supposed to be?

Don't fight what you can't control. Accept things and decide what you can and can't do about it. As you do, hold on to the idea that no matter what's going on in your life, you will always be guided to where you should be. You just have to believe that life happens for you, not to you.

Connections

Isn't it comforting to know that you haven't yet met
everyone who will come to love you?

Unexpected bonds

It's fascinating how someone you once didn't know at all can end up being such a big part of your life. At first, they're just another face in the crowd, but somehow, they stick around. They become the person you turn to for advice, for a laugh, or just to hang out. You start sharing your thoughts, your fears, your dreams with them. And before you know it, they're not just a friend, they're family. They're with you through thick and thin, celebrating your successes and supporting you through rough patches. You can't imagine your life without them. It's funny how someone who was once a total stranger can end up being so important.

Relationships

What if we aren't meant to be with one person for the rest of our lives? What if instead of a failed relationship it was a successful relationship for the time it lasted? Just because people stay together for a long period of time doesn't make a relationship successful.

Sparks

For a long time after the breakup, I felt awfully empty inside. My spark was gone and the light had dimmed. I thought I wouldn't be able to love again for a very long time. I could chat with all kinds of great guys – handsome, intelligent, and interesting – but I simply didn't feel anything. The fire inside me was gone.

But then, something about you quietly caught my attention. You stand out, not just in appearance; you are determined, capable, and yet down to earth, and that's incredibly attractive. It's a beautiful and thrilling feeling, a sensation I haven't had in a while. You've awakened something within me, and suddenly I am excited to love again someday.

Heartfelt rush

I couldn't help but feel a rush of excitement. Your words, your smile, everything about you seemed to make my heart skip a beat. You inspire me, you make me nervous, you make me feel alive in a way I haven't in a long time.

Nearby longing

You've become a presence in my daily life. Your passion and dedication to reaching your goals continue to inspire me. I admire your sense of style; you stand out from the crowd and you are incredibly handsome. I find myself captivated by you; you are so near, yet so out of reach.

Desire

I have an intense longing inside me that craves more, an undeniable desire to kiss you with passion.

Finding happiness

Isn't it funny how life is just somehow happening the way it's meant to be? It might be hard to believe in the moment, but when you look back it all makes sense. You have to learn to let go of what isn't right for you so that you can make space for what is.

Calm

I am feeling a sense of tranquillity within me.
I am calm. My breathing is steady.
I am relaxed. My body feels warm and light.
I am in peace. Everything is okay and there is nothing
to worry about.

Adventure

With a heart full of appreciation, I choose to embrace my journey, knowing that the laughter, the lessons, and the love are all part of this wonderfully imperfect adventure we call life.

Smile

Acknowledgements

First and foremost, I want to shamelessly thank myself for the dedication and effort I've poured into writing this book. It has been a journey of perseverance, and I'm grateful for every moment of it.

I am immensely thankful to my family for their constant support in everything I do and for instilling in me the belief that I can achieve anything I set my mind to. Your encouragement has been a pillar of strength throughout my entire life.

I would like to express my heartfelt gratitude to Laura and Amy for being wellsprings of inspiration for some of the words that found their way onto these pages.

To Lara, Hayley, and Laura, I extend my sincere thanks for taking the time to review the early drafts of this manuscript and for offering me your honest and vital feedback. Your input has been crucial in refining this work to its fullest potential.

Special thanks to Leah for her invaluable advice on book covers and to Sandra for her guidance on the nuances of self-publishing. Your expertise has been essential in managing the complexities of bringing this book to life.

Last but not least, I am incredibly grateful to my editor and proofreader, Abbie, for her detailed work and consistent dedication to refining this manuscript. Your keen eye and editorial insights have truly elevated this book to new heights.

Thank you for taking the time to read my book!
I hope you enjoyed the journey. If you could take a
moment to leave a review, I would greatly appreciate
it. Your feedback means a lot to me. Thank you!

www.ingramcontent.com/pod-product-compliance
Lightning Source LLC
Chambersburg PA
CBHW050028040726

47599CB00015B/1588